USBORNE BIG MACHINES
DIGGERS
AND CRANES

Caroline Young

Designed by Steve Page

Illustrated by Chris Lyon and Teri Gower

Additional illustrations by Nick Hawker
Cover design by Tom Lalonde

Consultant: D. Wheeler (Senior Plant Engineer,
George Wimpey Ltd.)

Contents

Bulldozers

Bulldozers clear the ground ready for building. They push earth, stones and tree stumps out of their way with a huge metal blade. This is called dozing.

Crawler tracks

Crawler tracks

Crawler tracks help the heavy bulldozer climb up steep banks.

They can go over bumps more smoothly than wheels, too.

They help stop the bulldozer sinking into soft, muddy ground.

This is where the driver sits. It is called a cab.

The cab has a frame of metal bars. They protect the driver if the bulldozer rolls over.

In hot countries, the cab has no glass in its windows. This keeps the driver cool.

Fire extinguisher

This bulldozer has a powerful engine. It can push things much heavier than itself.

This tool is called a ripper. It drags behind the bulldozer breaking up hard, stony ground.

Metal crawler tracks cover the bulldozer's wheels.

This metal arm is called a tilt ram. It pushes the bulldozer's blade up. This helps it pile up earth.

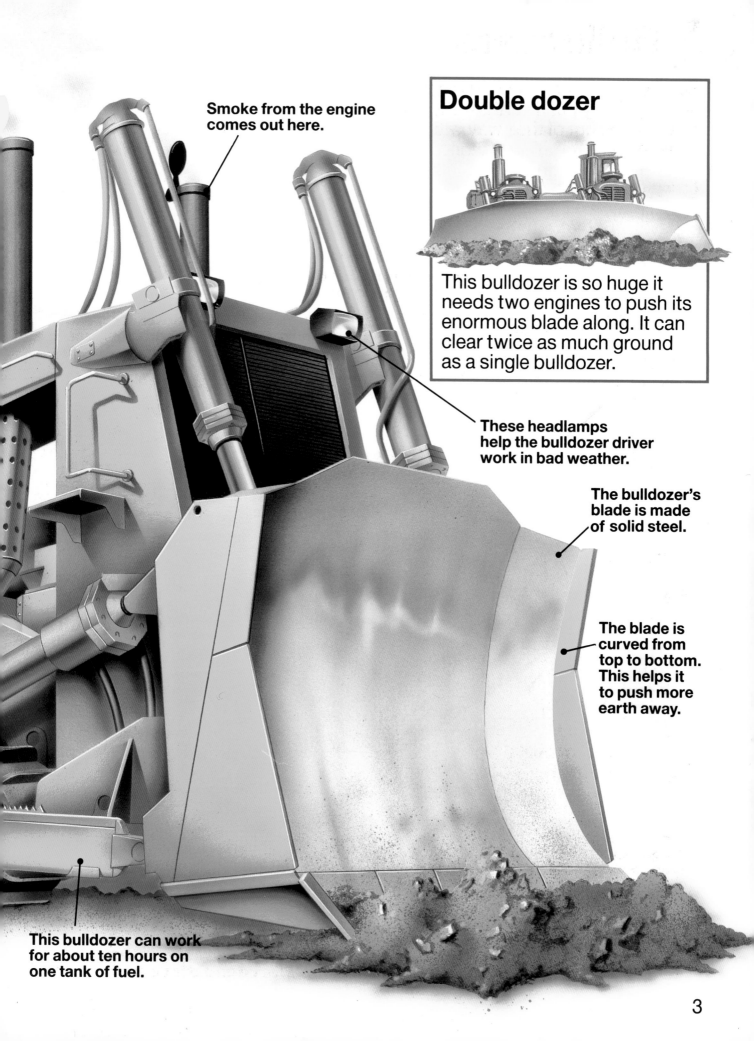

Smoke from the engine comes out here.

Double dozer

This bulldozer is so huge it needs two engines to push its enormous blade along. It can clear twice as much ground as a single bulldozer.

These headlamps help the bulldozer driver work in bad weather.

The bulldozer's blade is made of solid steel.

The blade is curved from top to bottom. This helps it to push more earth away.

This bulldozer can work for about ten hours on one tank of fuel.

3

Backhoe excavator

Digging machines are called excavators. There are lots of different sorts. Excavators can do other jobs, too. You can see some at work at the bottom of this page.

This digger is a backhoe excavator. It digs into the ground with a metal bucket called a backhoe.

These are rams. They slide in and out of their metal case. This makes the excavator's arm move.

This bucket can dig up more than 500 spadefuls of earth at a time.

This is the boom. The driver can make it shorter or longer for each digging job.

This is the dipper arm. It dips in and out of the ground as the excavator digs.

These metal teeth cut through the earth easily.

This mini-excavator is so small it could fit into the backhoe excavator's bucket. It does small digging jobs.

Other excavators

These excavators have tools that do many different jobs.

This excavator can carry earth in a loader bucket.

Claws help this excavator pick up pipes or logs.

This excavator's metal grab picks things up easily.

4

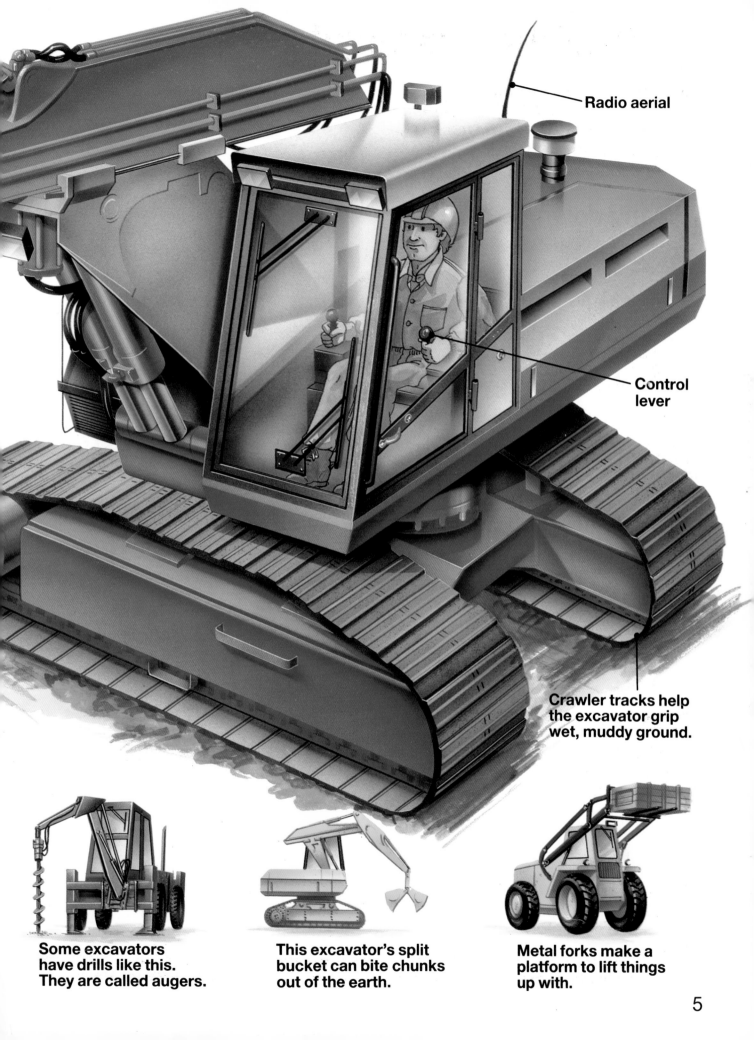

Radio aerial

Control lever

Crawler tracks help the excavator grip wet, muddy ground.

Some excavators have drills like this. They are called augers.

This excavator's split bucket can bite chunks out of the earth.

Metal forks make a platform to lift things up with.

5

Backhoe loader

This excavator can do many digging jobs. It can dig pits and trenches with a backhoe or scoop up earth in a bucket called a loader. It is called a backhoe loader.

Up and down

Backhoe

The backhoe can stretch up as high as an upstairs window to dig.

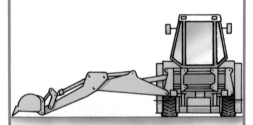

It can swivel around and dig at the side of the excavator, like this.

It can also reach down like this to scoop up earth and dig a trench.

The cab has glass all the way round. The driver has a good view as he controls the machine.

The driver can turn his seat to face the loader or the backhoe.

Headlight

This bucket is called the backhoe.

The driver uses these two levers to control the backhoe.

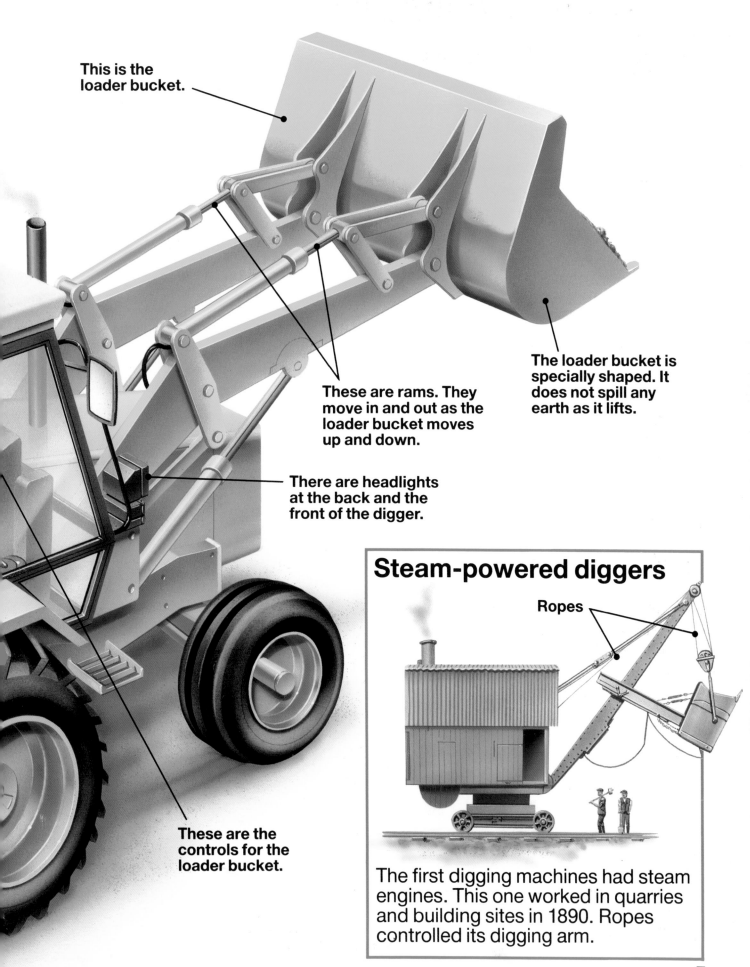

This is the loader bucket.

The loader bucket is specially shaped. It does not spill any earth as it lifts.

These are rams. They move in and out as the loader bucket moves up and down.

There are headlights at the back and the front of the digger.

These are the controls for the loader bucket.

Steam-powered diggers

Ropes

The first digging machines had steam engines. This one worked in quarries and building sites in 1890. Ropes controlled its digging arm.

Moving cranes

These cranes move around on wheels or crawler tracks. They are called truck cranes and crawler cranes. They can move quickly from job to job.

The arm a crane lifts with is called a jib or a boom.

This boom has four parts. They fold away inside each other like this when the crane is not lifting.

Ready to lift

Boom

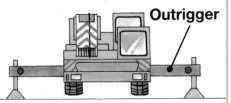

The truck crane arrives at the building site with its boom folded up.

Outrigger

Metal legs called outriggers lift the crane off the ground.

The boom slowly lifts up and slides out ready to lift a load.

Truck crane

Truck cranes are built on the back of a truck.

When it slides out, this boom can stretch up to the top of a six floor building.

A truck crane has two cabs. One is for driving the truck. The other is to control the crane.

Crane cab

The crane's engine is under here.

This is an outrigger. It supports the crane while it is lifting.

Outriggers slide away underneath the truck crane when it is not lifting.

The crane's wheels are not touching the ground.

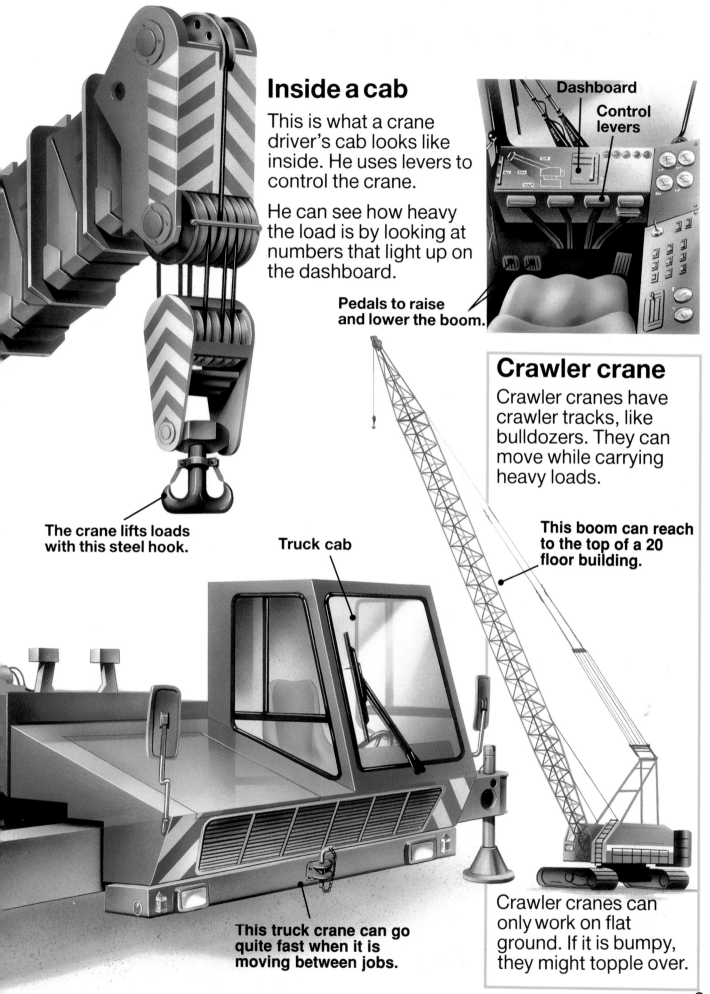

Inside a cab

This is what a crane driver's cab looks like inside. He uses levers to control the crane.

He can see how heavy the load is by looking at numbers that light up on the dashboard.

Dashboard

Control levers

Pedals to raise and lower the boom.

The crane lifts loads with this steel hook.

Truck cab

Crawler crane

Crawler cranes have crawler tracks, like bulldozers. They can move while carrying heavy loads.

This boom can reach to the top of a 20 floor building.

This truck crane can go quite fast when it is moving between jobs.

Crawler cranes can only work on flat ground. If it is bumpy, they might topple over.

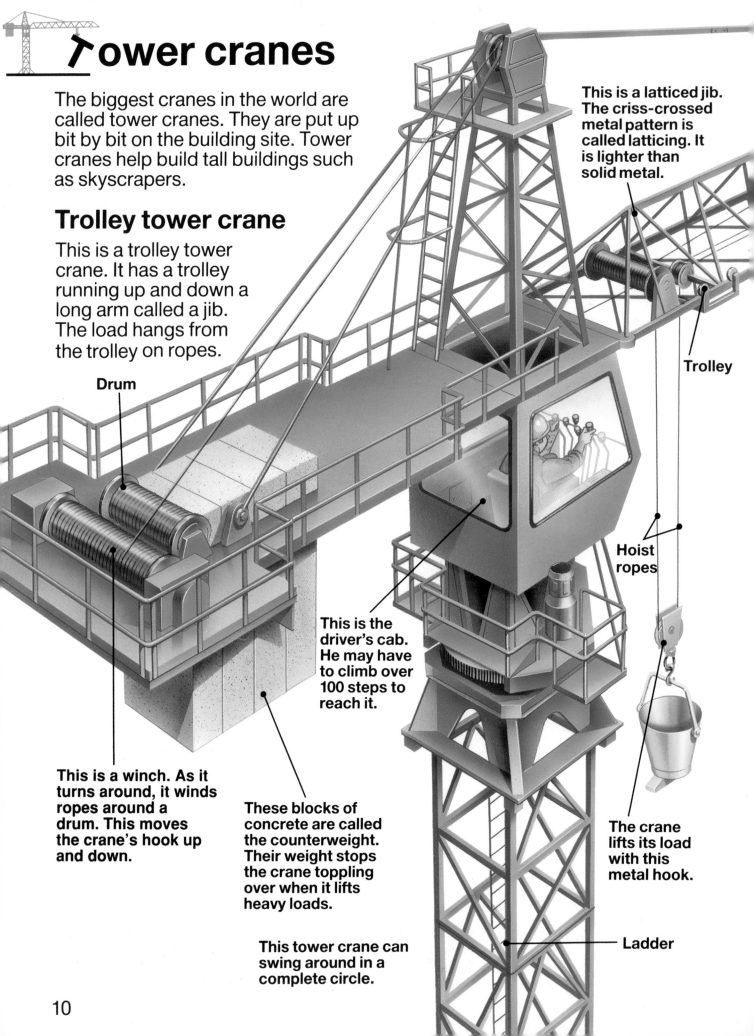

Tower cranes

The biggest cranes in the world are called tower cranes. They are put up bit by bit on the building site. Tower cranes help build tall buildings such as skyscrapers.

Trolley tower crane

This is a trolley tower crane. It has a trolley running up and down a long arm called a jib. The load hangs from the trolley on ropes.

This is a latticed jib. The criss-crossed metal pattern is called latticing. It is lighter than solid metal.

Trolley

Drum

Hoist ropes

This is the driver's cab. He may have to climb over 100 steps to reach it.

This is a winch. As it turns around, it winds ropes around a drum. This moves the crane's hook up and down.

These blocks of concrete are called the counterweight. Their weight stops the crane toppling over when it lifts heavy loads.

The crane lifts its load with this metal hook.

Ladder

This tower crane can swing around in a complete circle.

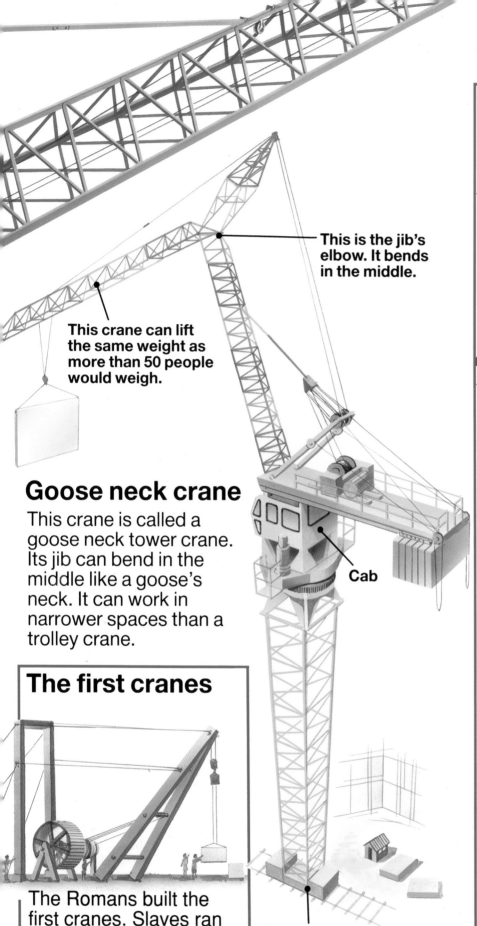

This is the jib's elbow. It bends in the middle.

This crane can lift the same weight as more than 50 people would weigh.

Cab

Goose neck crane

This crane is called a goose neck tower crane. Its jib can bend in the middle like a goose's neck. It can work in narrower spaces than a trolley crane.

The first cranes

The Romans built the first cranes. Slaves ran around inside a wooden wheel with ropes tied to it. This lifted things up.

The crane rests on heavy metal rails. Concrete blocks hold it in place.

Bit by bit

Trucks bring the parts of the tower crane to the building site.

A truck crane lifts the pieces of the tower crane into place.

Builders bolt the bits of the crane's jib together on the ground.

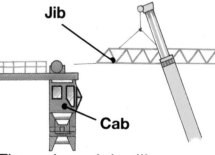

Jib

Cab

The cab and the jib are lifted into place by the truck crane.

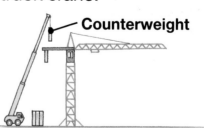

Counterweight

The truck crane lifts the counterweight. Now the crane is ready to work.

uilding roads 1

A lot of machines build a road. The ones you can see on this page get the ground ready.

Scraper

This is a scraper. It scrapes the top, bumpy layer off the ground.

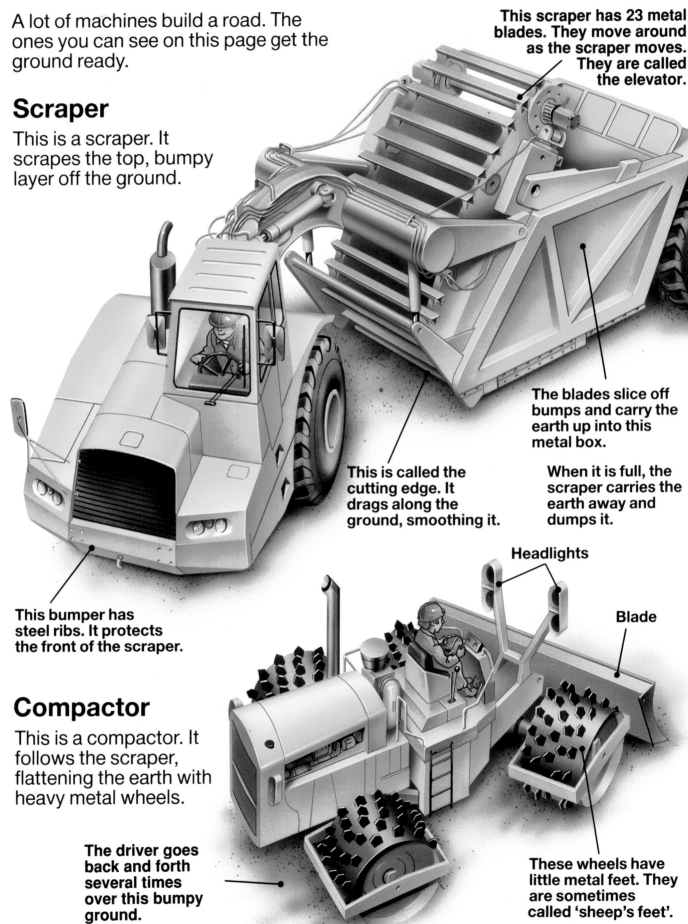

This scraper has 23 metal blades. They move around as the scraper moves. They are called the elevator.

The blades slice off bumps and carry the earth up into this metal box.

When it is full, the scraper carries the earth away and dumps it.

This is called the cutting edge. It drags along the ground, smoothing it.

This bumper has steel ribs. It protects the front of the scraper.

Compactor

This is a compactor. It follows the scraper, flattening the earth with heavy metal wheels.

Headlights

Blade

The driver goes back and forth several times over this bumpy ground.

These wheels have little metal feet. They are sometimes called 'sheep's feet'.

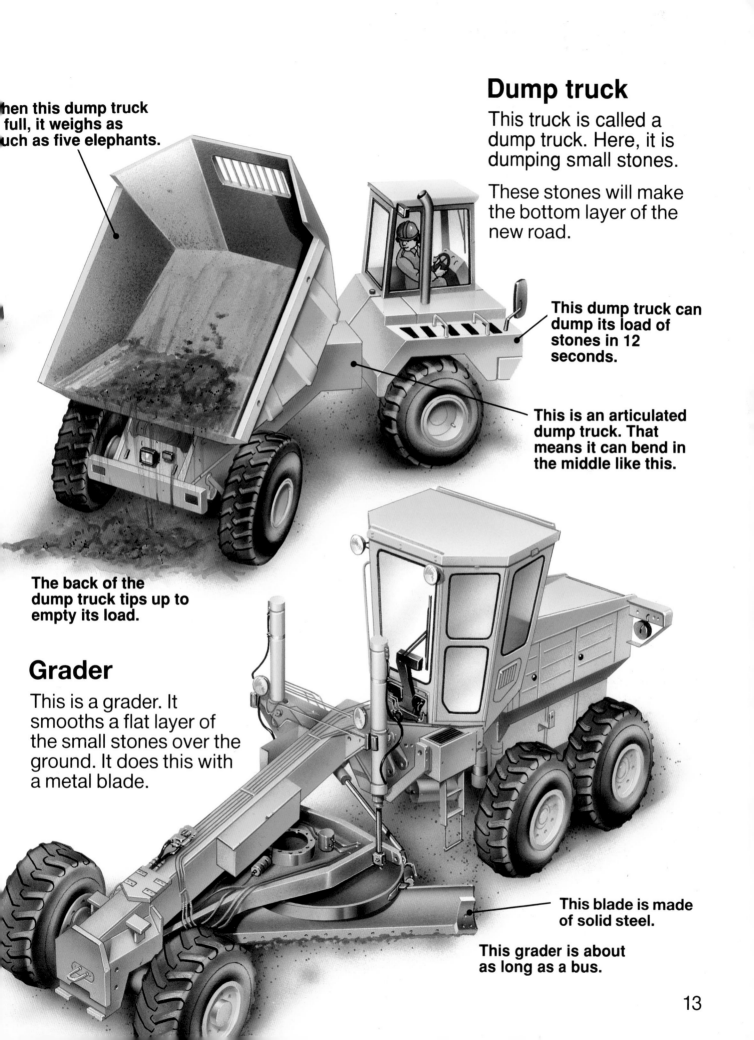

Dump truck

This truck is called a dump truck. Here, it is dumping small stones.

These stones will make the bottom layer of the new road.

**hen this dump truck
full, it weighs as
uch as five elephants.**

This dump truck can dump its load of stones in 12 seconds.

This is an articulated dump truck. That means it can bend in the middle like this.

The back of the dump truck tips up to empty its load.

Grader

This is a grader. It smooths a flat layer of the small stones over the ground. It does this with a metal blade.

This blade is made of solid steel.

This grader is about as long as a bus.

13

Building roads 2

A paver lays a mixture of hot tar and small stones on the road. A roller makes sure the road is flat.

Roller

This roller drives slowly behind the paver. It flattens the tar and stones with its heavy metal rollers.

It will go over the road several times to make it ready for cars and trucks to drive on it.

Steam rollers

The first rollers were called steam rollers. They had engines powered by steam. This steam roller was built in about 1847. It went very slowly.

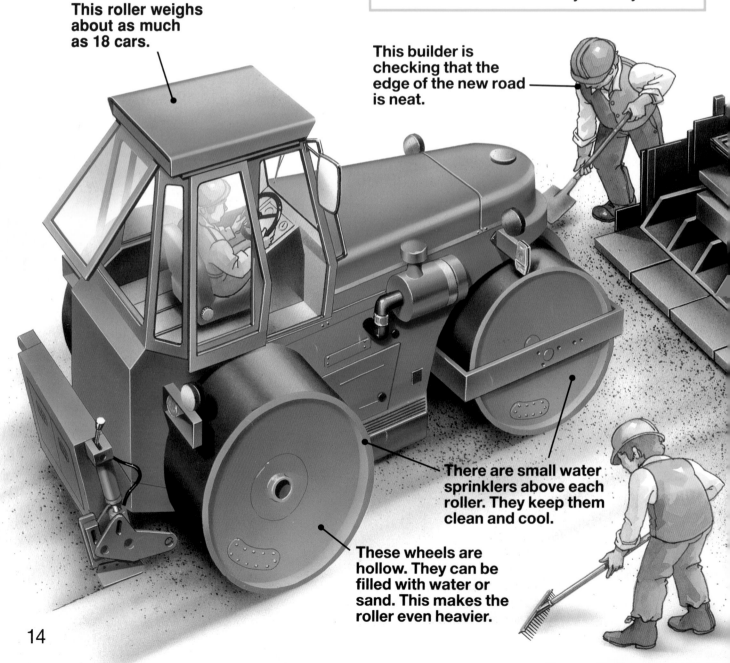

This roller weighs about as much as 18 cars.

This builder is checking that the edge of the new road is neat.

There are small water sprinklers above each roller. They keep them clean and cool.

These wheels are hollow. They can be filled with water or sand. This makes the roller even heavier.

Paver

A mixture of hot tar and small stones is called asphalt. A paver spreads a layer of warm asphalt over the road. It sets hard as it cools.

Filling up

A truck tips asphalt into a box called a hopper. It is at the front of the paver.

The asphalt goes through the paver and comes out of the back as it moves.

The truck can fill the paver with asphalt while it works.

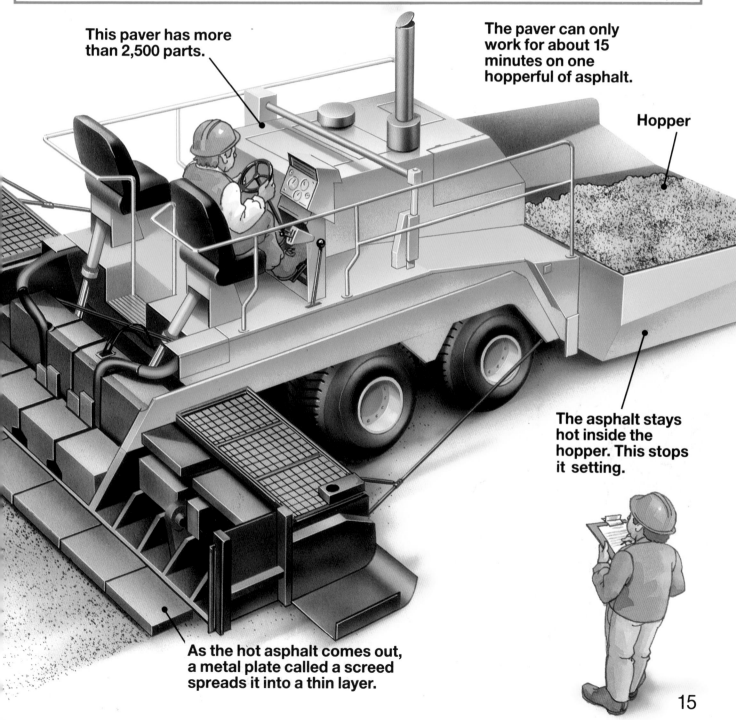

This paver has more than 2,500 parts.

The paver can only work for about 15 minutes on one hopperful of asphalt.

Hopper

The asphalt stays hot inside the hopper. This stops it setting.

As the hot asphalt comes out, a metal plate called a screed spreads it into a thin layer.

15

At the docks

Lots of different cranes work at the docks. Some are specially built to lift loads on and off ships. Others move cargo from place to place.

Container cranes

Many cargoes come in metal boxes, or containers. Cranes called container cranes can pick them up.

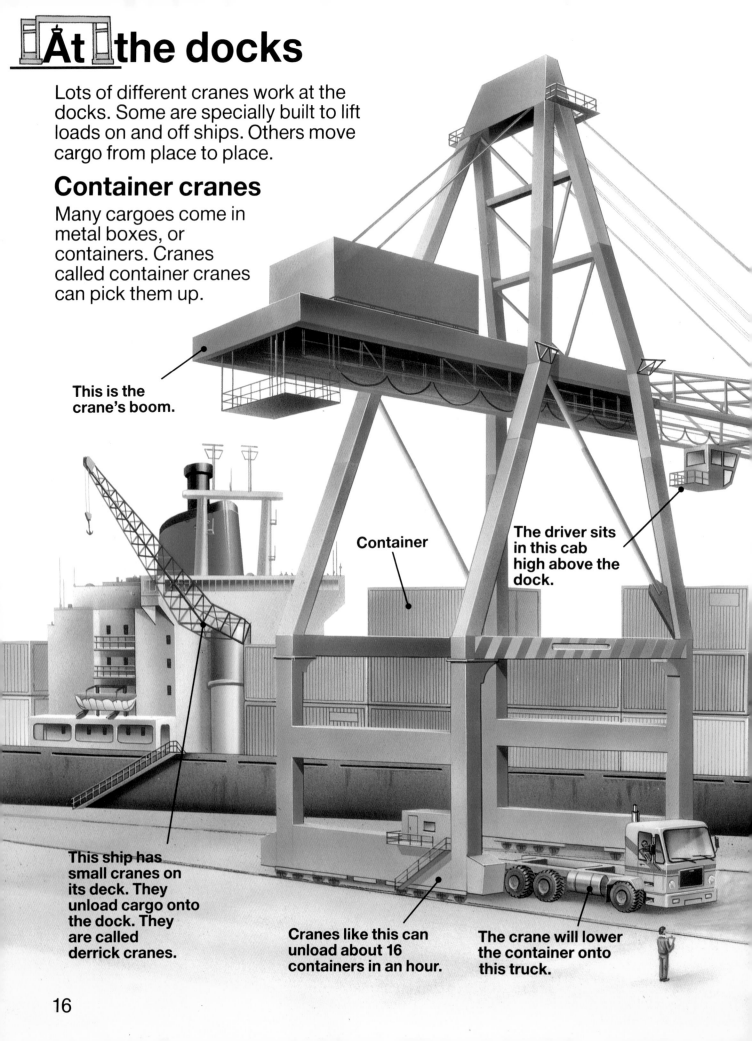

This is the crane's boom.

Container

The driver sits in this cab high above the dock.

This ship has small cranes on its deck. They unload cargo onto the dock. They are called derrick cranes.

Cranes like this can unload about 16 containers in an hour.

The crane will lower the container onto this truck.

16

Carrying containers

Boom

Trolley

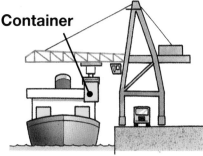

Container

The crane's boom is above the ship. Ropes and clamps hang down from a trolley.

The clamps grab the edges of the container. The driver pulls a lever and ropes lift it up.

The trolley slides back along the boom. The ropes slowly lower the container onto a truck.

Several container cranes work side by side at big docks.

Each of these containers is taller than two people standing on each others' shoulders.

Straddle Carrier

This crane is called a straddle carrier. It picks up containers and drives them away to stack them up.

This crane can stack four containers on top of each other.

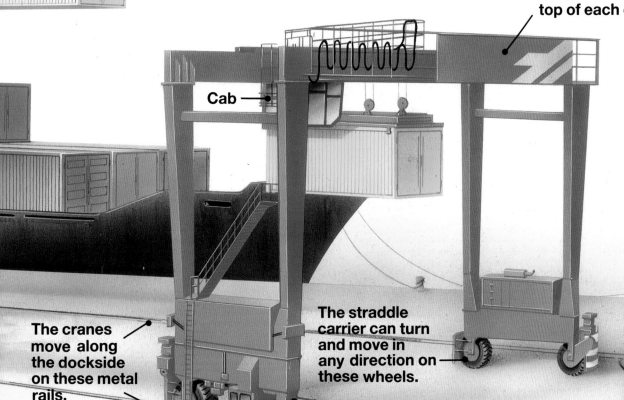

Cab

The cranes move along the dockside on these metal rails.

The straddle carrier can turn and move in any direction on these wheels.

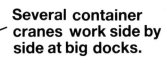

Building machines

Tall buildings are very heavy. The ground must be strong to hold them up. These machines are drilling holes in the ground and filling them with concrete and steel rods. This will strengthen the ground.

Underground legs

First a crane drills a hole in the ground with a tool called an auger. It is fixed to the crane's jib.

—Auger

Then a mobile crane lowers long steel rods down into each hole. They make steel 'legs'.

Concrete comes out here.

A concrete pump fills the holes with concrete. Now the ground is strong enough to build on.

Concrete mixer

The hollow drum on the back of a concrete mixer can turn around. It has metal blades inside it to mix concrete.

The drum turns around about eight times a minute to mix concrete.

The chalk, stones and sand to make concrete are poured in here.

Water to make concrete is in this tank.

The builder controls the mixer's drum with levers.

Concrete pours out of this metal tube.

18

Mini-mixer

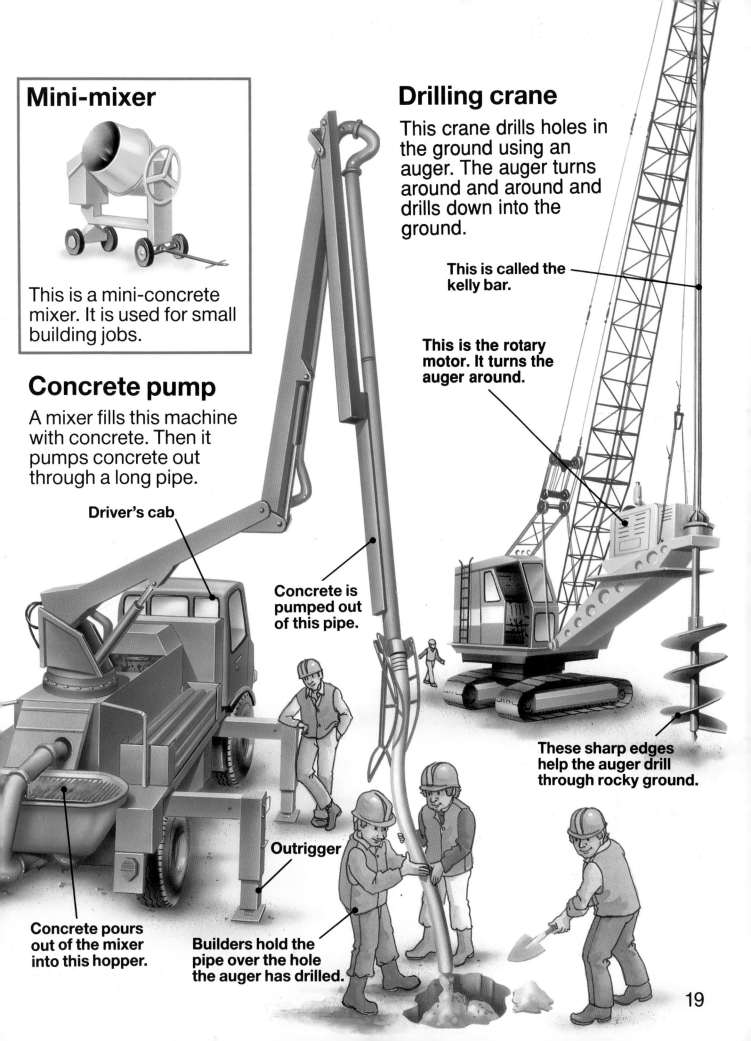

This is a mini-concrete mixer. It is used for small building jobs.

Concrete pump

A mixer fills this machine with concrete. Then it pumps concrete out through a long pipe.

Driver's cab

Concrete is pumped out of this pipe.

Concrete pours out of the mixer into this hopper.

Outrigger

Builders hold the pipe over the hole the auger has drilled.

Drilling crane

This crane drills holes in the ground using an auger. The auger turns around and around and drills down into the ground.

This is called the kelly bar.

This is the rotary motor. It turns the auger around.

These sharp edges help the auger drill through rocky ground.

19

Mining machines

Here are some of the diggers that work in mines. They dig up valuable things like coal, copper and gold. Some work underground and others dig on the earth's surface.

Bucket wheel excavator

Sometimes, coal is buried only just under the ground. This huge machine digs it up. It is called a bucket wheel excavator.

These wires lower the wheel until it is touching the ground.

Boom

The wheel turns around and around.

Buckets scrape up the coal as the wheel turns.

This sharp edge bites into the ground.

This excavator has 18 buckets. Each one can hold enough to fill a car with coal.

The wheel can scrape up about 40,000 bucketsful of coal in one day.

When all the coal is gone, people sometimes cover the mine with earth and plant grass again.

The driver sits in this cab to control the huge machine.

It takes five men to work this machine.

When they reach the top of the wheel, the buckets tip out their load. It falls onto a moving track inside the machine.

Underground mining

Things like coal and gold are often found deep under ground. Machines like these dig them up.

Pick

This machine cuts coal off the wall of the mine with blades called picks. It is called a continuous miner.

This is a coal face cutter. Its sharp blades slice coal off tunnel walls in mines.

Coal falls off the end of the track onto these waiting railway trucks.

This moving track carries the coal.

The excavator moves very slowly on huge crawler tracks.

Diggers and drills

People dig up stones and rock in quarries to use for building. They use these powerful machines.

Dragline excavator

This machine is called a dragline excavator. It can dig up much more than any other excavator in its huge steel bucket.

Boom

Dragging the bucket

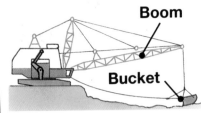

Boom

Bucket

The excavator has a bucket on the end of its boom. It lowers it onto the ground in front of it.

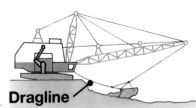

Dragline

Wires called draglines drag the bucket towards the excavator. It fills up with earth and rock.

When the bucket is full, the excavator empties it. Then the draglines let the bucket go again.

This bucket is big enough for a car to park inside it.

Dragline

Face shovel

A wall of solid rock is called a rock face. This machine digs into it. It is called a face shovel.

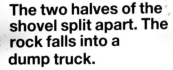

Crawler tracks hold the face shovel steady as it digs.

The two halves of the shovel split apart. The rock falls into a dump truck.

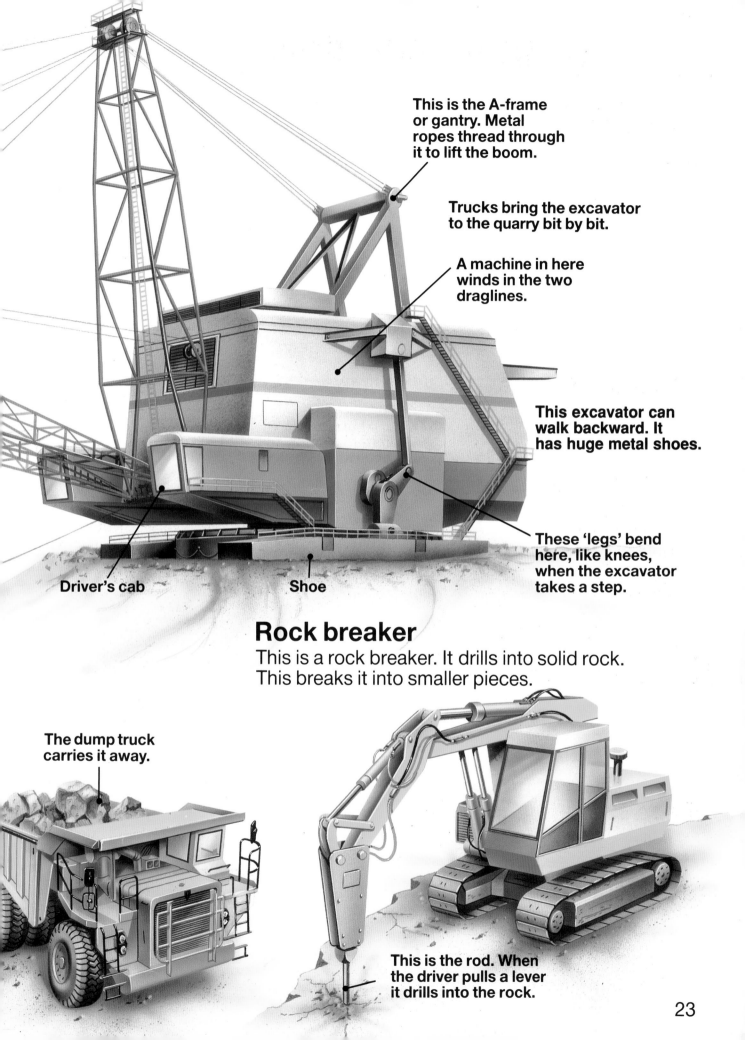

This is the A-frame or gantry. Metal ropes thread through it to lift the boom.

Trucks bring the excavator to the quarry bit by bit.

A machine in here winds in the two draglines.

This excavator can walk backward. It has huge metal shoes.

These 'legs' bend here, like knees, when the excavator takes a step.

Driver's cab

Shoe

Rock breaker

This is a rock breaker. It drills into solid rock. This breaks it into smaller pieces.

The dump truck carries it away.

This is the rod. When the driver pulls a lever it drills into the rock.

Floating diggers and cranes

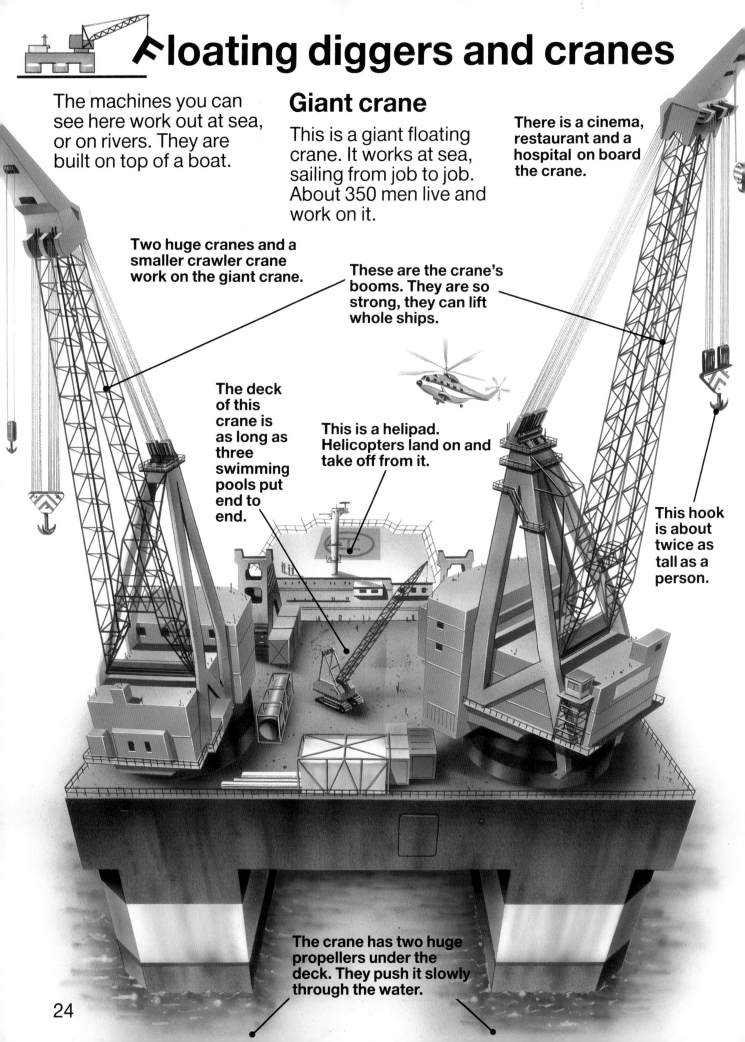

The machines you can see here work out at sea, or on rivers. They are built on top of a boat.

Giant crane

This is a giant floating crane. It works at sea, sailing from job to job. About 350 men live and work on it.

There is a cinema, restaurant and a hospital on board the crane.

Two huge cranes and a smaller crawler crane work on the giant crane.

These are the crane's booms. They are so strong, they can lift whole ships.

The deck of this crane is as long as three swimming pools put end to end.

This is a helipad. Helicopters land on and take off from it.

This hook is about twice as tall as a person.

The crane has two huge propellers under the deck. They push it slowly through the water.

Dredgers

Dredgers dig up mud and sand from the bottom of seas and rivers. This one is called a bucket dredger. It digs up mud in a chain of buckets called a ladder. They go around and around like a moving staircase.

How a dredger works

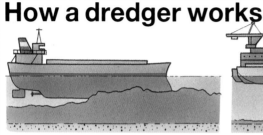

If mud builds up on the sea bed or a river bed, ships can get stuck on it.

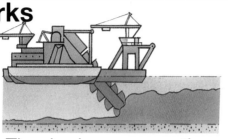

The dredger scoops the mud from the bottom and dumps it on barges.

The barges carry it out to sea. They dump it where the water is deep.

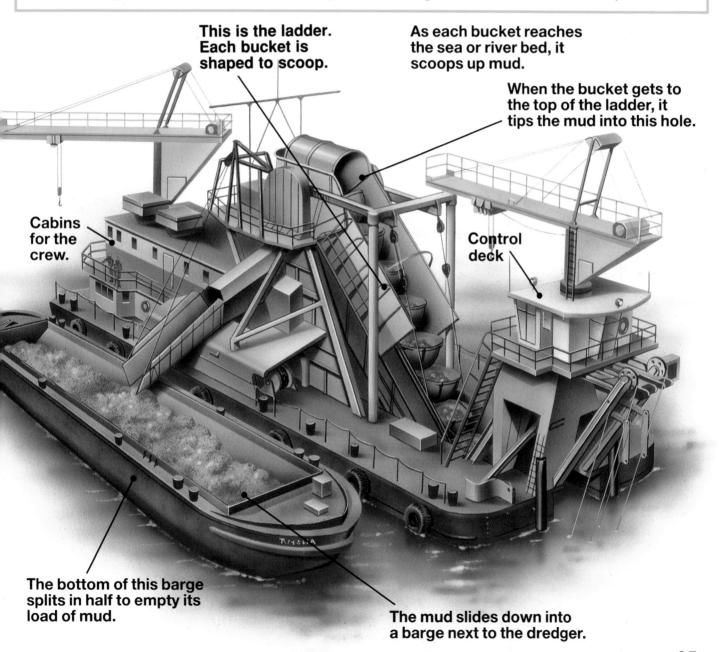

This is the ladder. Each bucket is shaped to scoop.

As each bucket reaches the sea or river bed, it scoops up mud.

When the bucket gets to the top of the ladder, it tips the mud into this hole.

Cabins for the crew.

Control deck

The bottom of this barge splits in half to empty its load of mud.

The mud slides down into a barge next to the dredger.

Tunnel diggers

Tunnelling machines have to be able to dig through earth, mud and even solid rock. The biggest tunnelling machines in the world are called TBMs. This stands for Tunnel Boring Machine.

Early tunnels

Builders covered the inside of the tunnel with bricks behind the machine.

This metal cage protected the men from falling earth.

This is one of the first tunnelling machines. It dug tunnels for underground trains in London over 170 years ago. Builders dug through earth with spades at the front as the machine moved forward.

A TBM

Tunnel Boring Machines like this one dug the Channel Tunnel under the sea between England and France. Here you can see what part of a TBM looks like inside.

The TBM grips the inside of the tunnel with four metal plates like these. They are called gripper shoes.

This is a segment erector. It covers the inside of the tunnel with concrete segments .

Cutterhead

The dug-out earth from the cutterhead is carried out on this moving belt.

The TBM has 20 rams like this. They push it forward as it digs.

This is the cutterhead. It spins around and cuts through the earth with sharp blades.

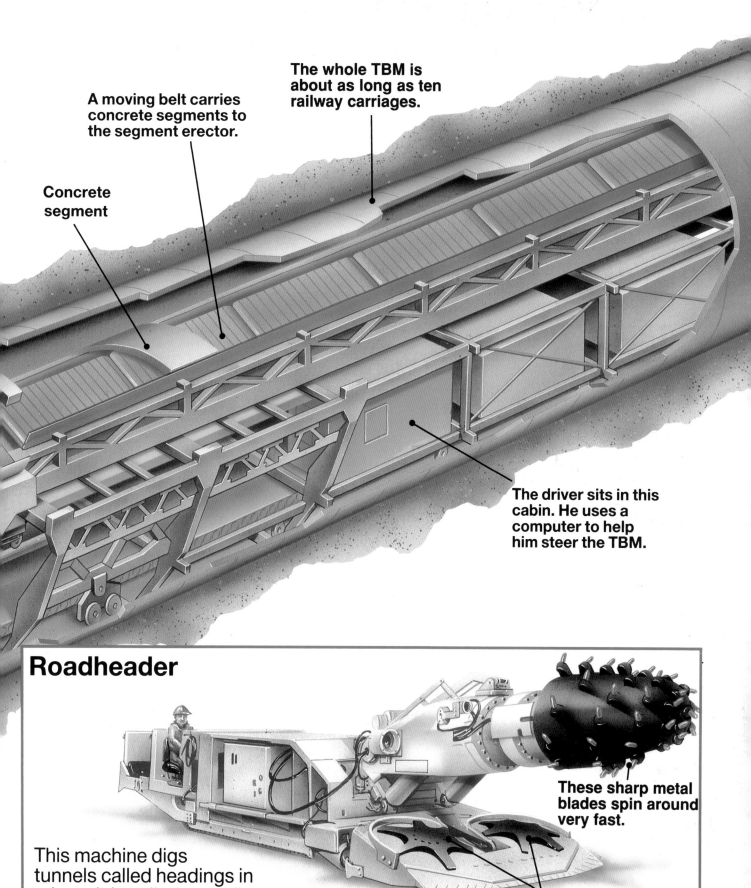

A moving belt carries concrete segments to the segment erector.

The whole TBM is about as long as ten railway carriages.

Concrete segment

The driver sits in this cabin. He uses a computer to help him steer the TBM.

Roadheader

This machine digs tunnels called headings in mines. It is called a roadheader. It has a sharp cutterhead covered with spiky blades which cut through rock.

These sharp metal blades spin around very fast.

These wheels spin. They push the rock into the machine and onto a moving belt.

Machine facts 1

On the next four pages are some facts about many of the machines in this book. They are medium-sized examples of each machine.

Bulldozer

Height: 3.5 m/11.5 ft
Length: 6.3 m/21 ft
Fastest speed: 10.5 kph/ 6.3 mph

Backhoe excavator

Boom

Height: 4 m/13 ft
Length: 3.5 m/11.5 ft
Length of boom: 2.4 m/ 8.5 ft

Backhoe loader

Height: 3 m/10 ft
Length: 6.18 m/20.5 ft
Deepest dig: 4.3 m/14 ft

Excavator with claws

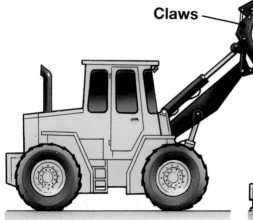

Claws

Height: 3 m/10 ft
Length: 6.2 m/25.5 ft
Number of claws: 2

Excavator with grab

Grab

Height: 3.2 m/10.5 ft
Length: 4.6 m/15 ft
Number of fingers: 5

Excavator with lifting forks

Height: 3 m/10 ft
Length: 6.2 m/20.5 ft
Highest stretch: 3.5 m/ 11.5 ft

Loader excavator

Height: 3.5 m/11.5 ft
Length: 7.3 m/24 ft
Bucket load: 10,360 kg/ 22,839 lbs

Scraper

Blade
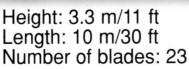

Height: 3.3 m/11 ft
Length: 10 m/30 ft
Number of blades: 23

Compactor

Height: 3.5 m/11.5 ft
Length: 6.8 m/22.5 ft
Weight: 20 tonnes/ 19.6 tons

Grader

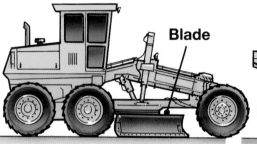

Height: 3.3 m/11 ft
Length: 7 m/23 ft
Length of blade: 4.2 m/
15 ft

Articulated dump truck

Height: 2.8 m/9 ft
Length: 6.5 m/21.5 ft
Biggest load: 12 tonnes/
11.8 tons

Heavy load dump truck

Height: 4 m/13 ft
Length: 9 m/30 ft
Biggest load: 55 tonnes/
54 tons

Roller

Height: 3 m/10 ft
Length: 5.2 m/18 ft
Biggest load: 10 tonnes/
9.8 tons

Paver

Height: 3 m/10 ft
Length: 5.9 m/19.5 ft
Fastest speed: 15 kph/
9.3 mph

Concrete mixer

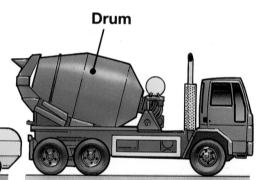

Height: 3.5 m/11.5 ft
Length: 5.9 m/19.5 ft
Drum speed: 12 turns per
minute

Concrete pump

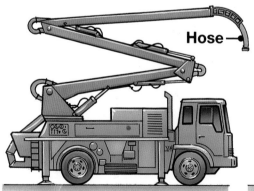

Height: 3 m/10 ft
Length: 8 m/26.5 ft
Full length of hose: 23 m/
76 ft

Rock breaker

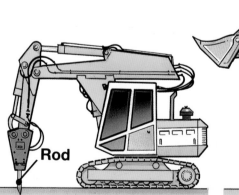

Height: 3.4 m/11 ft
Length of tracks: 3 m/10 ft
Length of rod: 0.6 m/2 ft

Power shovel

Height: 4.5 m/15 ft
Length: 6.3 m/21 ft
Highest stretch: 10 m/33 ft

Machine facts 2

Dragline excavator

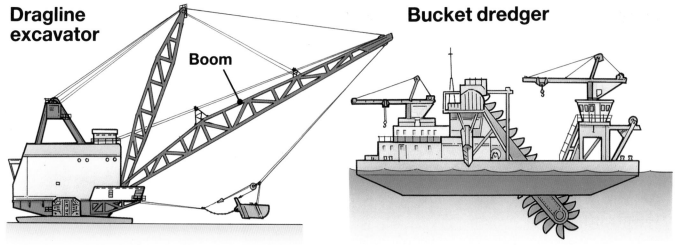

Boom

Height: 50 m/165 ft
Boom length: 79 m/261 ft
Crew: 2 people

Bucket dredger

Height: 23 m/76 ft
Length: 58 m/192 ft
Deepest dig: 25 m/83 ft

TBM (Tunnel Boring Machine)

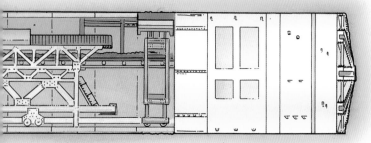

Height: 8.36 m/27.5 ft
Length: 220 m/726 ft
Digging speed: 6 m per
hour/20 ft per hour

Roadheader

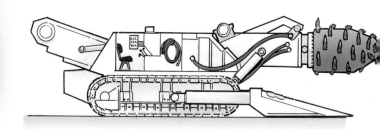

Height: 10 m/33 ft
Length: 9 m/30 ft
Weight: 42 tonnes/
41.3 tons

Continuous miner

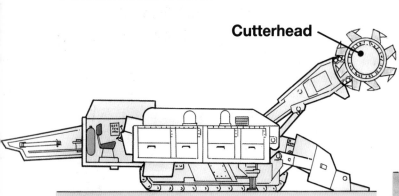

Cutterhead

Height: 1.5 m/5 ft
Length: 10.6 m/35 ft
Speed of cutterhead: 50
turns per minute

Bucket wheel excavator

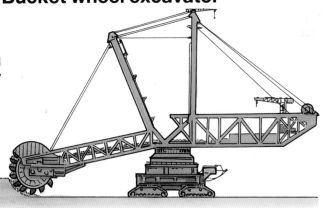

Number of buckets: 10
Deepest dig: 50 m/165 ft
Crew: 2 people

Crawler crane

Boom

Height: 4.3 m/14 ft
Length: 9.8 m/32 ft
Boom length: 80 m/264 ft

Tower crane

Goose neck crane

Jib

Section

Truck crane

Boom

Height: 3.8 m/12.5 ft
Length: 12 m/39.5 ft
Longest boom length:
35 m/ 116 ft

Height: 65 m/215 ft
Section height: 6 m/20 ft
Biggest load: 20 tonnes/
19.6 tons

Height: 104 m/334 ft
Jib length: 34 m/112 ft
Biggest load: 12 tonnes/
11.8 tons

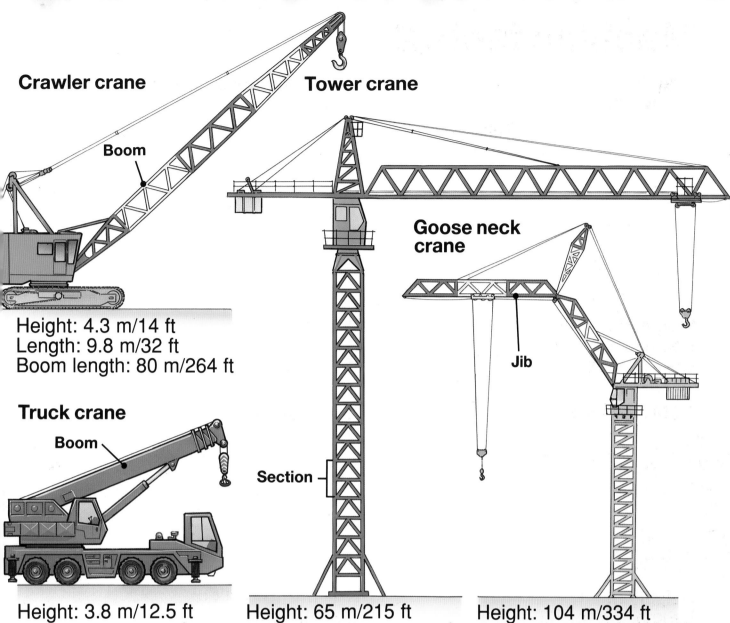

Container crane

Boom

Height: 60 m/198 ft
Boom length: 80 m/264 ft
Biggest load: 50 tonnes/
49.2 tons

Straddle carrier

Boom

Height: 12 m/39.5 ft
Boom length: 12 m/39.5 ft
Biggest load: 50 tonnes/
49.2 tons

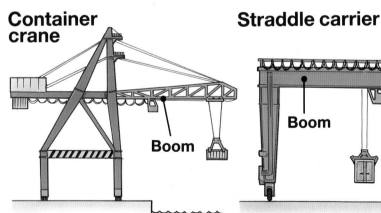

Giant floating crane

Boom

Length: 154 m/508 ft
Biggest load:
1,000 tonnes/984 tons
Number of booms: 2

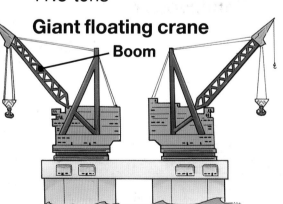

Index